Turquoise Jewelry

Nancy N. Schiffer

Revised and expanded 2nd edition

4880 Lower Valley Road, Atglen, PA 19310 USA

Acknowledgments

For their cooperation and kindness during the preparation of this book, I wish to thank several generous private collectors who prefer to remain anonymous, and Albert E. Anthony, Adobe Gallery, Albuquerque; Guy Berger, Palms Trading Company, Albuquerque; Margarete and Fred Chase, Enchanted Mesa Indian Arts, Albuquerque; Bing Crosby, Bing Crosby Arts and Crafts, Albuquerque; Tommy Elkins and Willa and Tom Bastien, Indian Traders West, Santa Fe; Carolyn Foreback, Indian Post, Allentown, Pa.; Connie, David, and Wayne Nez Gaussoin, Santa Fe; Cathren and Mary Harris, Turquoise Lady, Albuquerque; Harold L. James at the Montana Bureau of Mines, Butte; Lindsay D. Johnson and Leonard D. Prins at Prins and Volkhardt Jewelers, Strafford, Pa.; Walter Kennedy, Dennehotso collection, Kirtland, N.M.; Jane Calvert Love at the New Mexico Bureau of Mine and Mineral Resources, Socorro; Nancy Peake; Marian Rodee, curator, Maxwell Museum of the University of New Mexico, Albuquerque; Bruce Waters, Herbert and Peter Schiffer for their help with the photographs; Tim Scott for his wonderful photography and editorial assistance; Lynn D. Trusdell, Crown and Eagle Antiques, Inc., New Hope, Pa.; Tom Woodard, Santa Fe, N.M.; Margaret and Barton Wright.

Cover: Turquoise and lapis bead necklace of 10 strands, Navajo, circa 1985. Zuni 10 row cuff bracelet of matching petit point turquoise, circa 1940. 3-stone matching turquoise cuff bracelet, sterling silver. Navajo, circa 1910. 14K gold necklace with turquoise pendant by Paul Avriso, Navajo, circa 1995. Zuni channel inlay link bracelet of silver, turquoise, shell, onyx, and coral, circa 1990. Private collection.

Opposite: Sterling silver and Kingman turquoise necklace by Corbet Joe, Navajo. $300 / Cuff bracelet with silver, coral, and turquoise inlay by Ethel Martinez, Navajo. $200 / Turquoise and silver ring by D.K. Lister, Navajo. $100 / Roadrunner pin in silver with turquoise, circa 1985, $55. Leonard D. Prins collection.

Please note: The value ranges that appear here are derived from compiled sources and were not supplied by the people acknowledged in the credit lines. The ranges were conscientiously determined to reflect the market at the time this work was compiled. No responsibility for their future accuracy is accepted by the author, the publisher, or the people credited with the photographs.

Revised price guide and expanded second edition: 2004
Copyright © 1990 & 2004 by Schiffer Publishing, Ltd.
Library of Congress Control Number: 2004103983

Designed by "Sue"
Typeset in PhyllisD/Korinna BT

ISBN: 0-7643-2033-5
Printed in China
1 2 3 4

Published by Schiffer Publishing Ltd.
4880 Lower Valley Road
Atglen, PA 19310
Phone: (610) 593-1777; Fax: (610) 593-2002
E-mail: Info@schifferbooks.com

For the largest selection of fine reference books on this and related subjects, please visit our web site at
www.schifferbooks.com
We are always looking for people to write books on new and related subjects. If you have an idea for a book please contact us at the above address.

This book may be purchased from the publisher.
Include $3.95 for shipping.
Please try your bookstore first.
You may write for a free catalog.

In Europe, Schiffer books are distributed by
Bushwood Books
6 Marksbury Ave.
Kew Gardens
Surrey TW9 4JF England
Phone: 44 (0) 20 8392-8585;
Fax: 44 (0) 20 8392-9876
E-mail: info@bushwoodbooks.co.uk
Free postage in the U.K., Europe; air mail at cost.

Contents

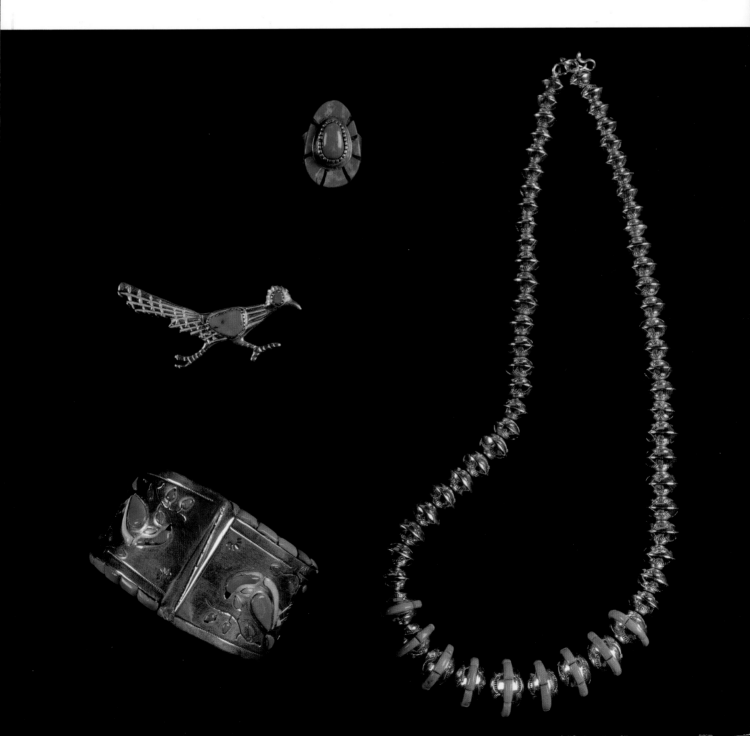

Zuni needlepoint turquoise and silver link bracelet. $150 / Two old style silver hairpins. $80-100 pr. / Large petit point round pin, Zuni, $120. Turquoise Lady collection.

Fine link-set necklace and cuff bracelet with turquoise by Glenda Emsato, Zuni, circa 1980s. $350 / Necklace with ten strands of fine turquoise and coral beads by Benny Aguilar, Santo Domingo, circa 1980s, $375. Indian Post collection.

Turquoise in History

The lovely blue and green color tones of turquoise have made it a favorite ornament of many civilizations. Its name is derived from French meaning "turkish stone" because it was first introduced from Persia to Europe through trade routes across Turkey. Egyptians are known to have used decorative turquoise from the Sinai peninsula by 3200 B.C.

On the American continents, the use of turquoise for personal decoration has been verified by the large amounts found during excavations at Pueblo Bonito in Chaco Canyon, New Mexico which date to approximately 777 A.D. These findings include beads, pendants, carved birds, and mosaics made from turquoise which probably originated in mines of the Cerillos area of New Mexico. Turquoise was apparently an important trade item, for New Mexican turquoise reached Mexico City, the Mayan cities and the Aztecs. A very old mosaic plaque set with 3,000 pieces of turquoise of New Mexico origin was found at Chichen Itza, Yucatan.

When Spanish explorers looking for gold traveled into the present-day American Southwest in the mid-sixteenth century, they recorded that the native people they met had turquoise beads, pendants and inlay for personal adornment, house decorations and items of trade.[1]

Anglo prospectors and settlers who came to the Southwest from the East in the mid-nineteenth century, rediscovered some of the old turquoise mines and organized a new trade in turquoise. By the early nineteenth century, many of the old mines had been exhausted and active searching for new sources brought discoveries of turquoise in isolated areas. White traders who encouraged jewelry making also imported turquoise. From 1890, Juan Lorenzo Hubble obtained Persian turquoise for silversmiths at his trading post at Ganado.

Imitation and Enhanced Turquoise

As the demand for turquoise has increased from time to time over the last seventy-five years, beyond the possibility of being satisfied by natural material, imitation turquoise has been developed. Sometimes this imitation material has been in the form of artificially colored natural stone, and sometimes as an outright imitation in texture as well as color. Enhancement of turquoise is not a new idea. In the thirteenth century, Persians applied butter or mutton fat tot he stone to deepen its color.[2] In America, Santo Domingo pueblo Indians in ancient time oiled their stones.[3] Legally, no harm has been done as long as the imitation is correctly identified as such. But a buyer should know that imitations do exist, and should ask for assurances if they have any doubt.

A new material called "rainbow calsilica" has appeared in some Native American jewelry in the American Southwest. This material is striped in many colors and has been used like other stones to enhance silver jewelry. When presented to gem analysis laboratories for identification, rainbow calsilica has been classified as having man-made properties colored with man-made pigments stabilized with epoxy.[4]

Rainbow Calsilica

A new material called "rainbow calsilica" has appeared in some Native American jewelry in the American Southwest. This material from Chihuahua, Mexico, is striped in many colors and has been used like other stones to enhance silver jewelry. When presented to gem analysis laboratories for identification, rainbow calsilica has been classified as having man-made properties colored with man-made pigments stabilized with epoxy.[4]

[1] Stuart A. Northrop, *Minerals of New Mexico* (Albuquerque: University of New Mexico Press, 1959), p. 533.
[2] *Ibid*, p. 534.
[3] Carl Rosneck and Joseph Stacey, *Skystone and Silver: The Collector's Book of Southwest Indian Jewelry* (Englewood Cliffs, N.J.: Prentice-Hall, Inc., 1976), p. 45.
[4] Robert Weldon, "Something Over the Rainbow," Professional Jeweler, Sept. 2003, p. 44.

Two sterling silver bracelets set with a pale, absorbent mineral dyed blue to resemble turquoise, by Maisel. / The triple line bracelet is machine stamped, circa 1930s. $140 / The other is "Howelite," circa 1970s-1980s, $85. Dennehotso collection.

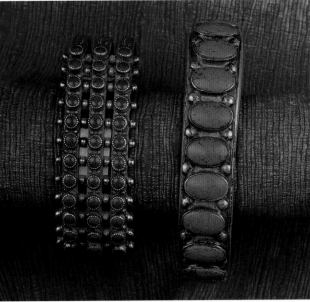

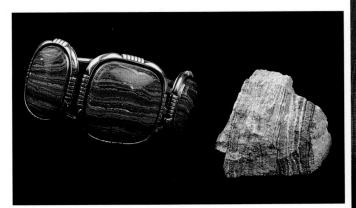

Bracelet with three rainbow calsilica stones by Lonnie Willie, and an unpolished calsilica nugget. Courtesy of Palms Trading Company, Albuquerque. $225-300

In desert areas of the world, where copper is mined, turquoise is generally found at shallow depths, usually not below about 100 feet. Ancient mining was accomplished with hand tools and in alluvial deposits not far from the sources. When referring to turquoise from particular areas or mines, the name of the mine is usually mentioned. The nature of turquoise veins include the surrounding rocks as the matrix which often become mixed with turquoise and present variations in its appearance. Mines also produce turquoise in a variety of densities, porosity, and colors. The dominant features of turquoise from particular mines are mentioned below.

In New Mexico, possibly the oldest Southwest turquoise mines were in the **Cerillos** hills, twenty miles south of the present-day Santa Fe, and in particular at the mountain which the Spanish called Mount Chalchihuiti. Here, Pueblo Indians had for hundreds of years mined turquoise for ornamentation and an important trade item. Soon after their domination of the region, the Spanish took over authority of the mines and forced the Pueblo people to labor in the mines against their will. This practice, a mining accident which claimed many Indian lives, and the Spaniards' compelling introduction of Christianity contributed to the Indian revolt in 1680 which forced the Spanish to flee or be killed.[5]

In 1858, Blake, writing in the *American Journal of Science*, described the ancient Carillos excavation as extending to a depth of 200 feet and a width of more than 300 feet, "at the bottom pine trees over a hundred years old are now growing. This great excavation is made in the solid rock, and tens of thousands of tons of rock have been broken out."[6] Cerillos turquoise is usually soft blue or greenish, and often with a brown matrix.

Not far from Mount Chalchihuiti is Turquoise Hill where ancient mines were probably reopened in the 1870s, and where the American Turquoise Company took over mining operations in 1892.[7] Because the Tiffany family of New York were principle stockholders of this company, the most successful mine here was named the **Tiffany**,[8] and another is the **Castillian** mine. Commercial mining continued here until 1925 when the turquoise supply was exhausted.

Elsewhere in New Mexico, in the southwest corner of the state, are turquoise mines in the **Burro** Mountains near Tyrone which were discovered in 1875 and produced a good quantity of high-grade turquoise in 1893. Near the **Hachita** Mountains is the Eureka area where turquoise was found in 1885 by prospectors looking for gold.[9] And a small mine at **Santa Rita** has produced some fine quality turquoise.

[5] Joseph E. Pogue, *Turquoise* (Glorieta, N.M.: The Rio Grande Press, Inc., 1975), p. 53; and Northrop, *Minerals*, p. 530.
[6] Pogue, *Turquois*, p. 52.
[7] *Ibid*, p. 53.
[8] Robert H. Weber, "Turquoise in New Mexico," *New Mexico Geology*, vol. 1, no. 3, August 1979, p. 39.
[9] *Ibid*, p. 39.

NEW MEXICO

Cerillos turquoise bracelet, ring, and earrings set, $450. Turquoise Lady collection.

In Arizona, turquoise is found in four widely scattered areas. The **Kingman** mine, near the town by the same name in the western part of the state, has produced light to dark colored turquoise and a great deal that is treated. The **Bisbee** mine, near the town of Bisbee in the southern area of the state, has been an important producer of dark blue turquoise with black or red veining. Here, the best quality comes from a section of a copper mine known as the Lavender Pit. At **Morenci**, near the eastern border, turquoise deposits have yielded large quantities of light to dark blue stones with a light tan matrix. At **Castle Dome** and the **Pinto Valley** mine in the center of the state, most of the turquoise yield is used for treated stone, as the color is usually light blue.

ARIZONA

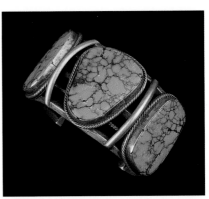

Navajo bracelet with old stabilized Kingman (Arizona) turquoise, 1960s to 1970s. $375-425

Bolo tie, buckle, watchband, and ring forming a man's set with Kingman turquoise and silver, circa 1970. $600-750. Private collection.

Bracelet with 2500 carat Morenci (Arizona) turquoise set in silver, made by Felecita Sandoval, Navajo. 6 1/4" long x 3" wide.

Bracelet of sterling silver with natural Sleeping Beauty (Arizona) turquoise, 1995, by David Gaussoin, Picuris Pueblo and Navajo. Courtesy of David Gaussoin

7

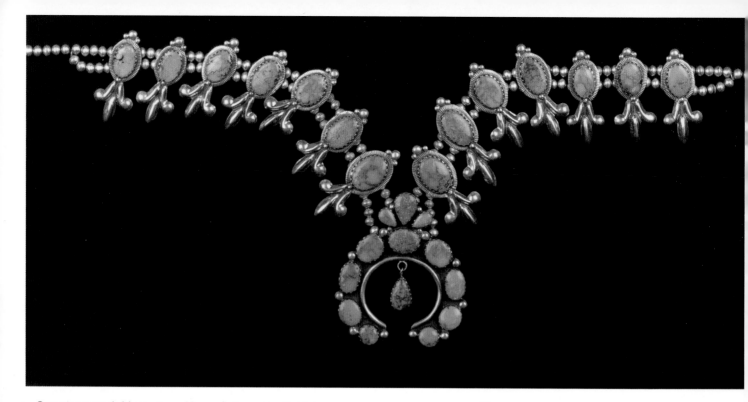

Superior squash blossom necklace of silver set with high quality Morenci turquoise, circa 1976. $1500. Private collection on permanent loan to Ohio University.

Kingman turquoise man's set featuring bolo tie, watchband, buckle, tie tac, ring, and cufflinks. Watchband, bolo tie, and buckle by Bernice and Robert Leekya, Zuni. $1000-1200. Private collection.

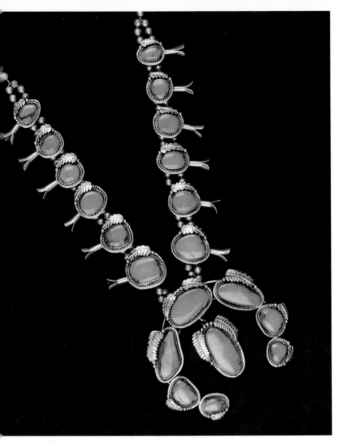

Large Bisbee turquoise "hip hugger" squash blossom necklace with handmade beads, a 6 3/8-inch-wide naja, and 39 1/2-inch total length. $1800. Private collection.

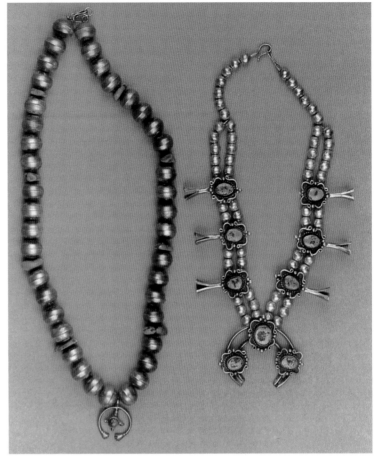

Two sterling silver and treated Kingman turquoise necklaces: The squash blossom style with nine stones, circa 1960s. $700-800 / The bead necklace with a spincast naja, circa 1970. $400-500. Dennehotso collection.

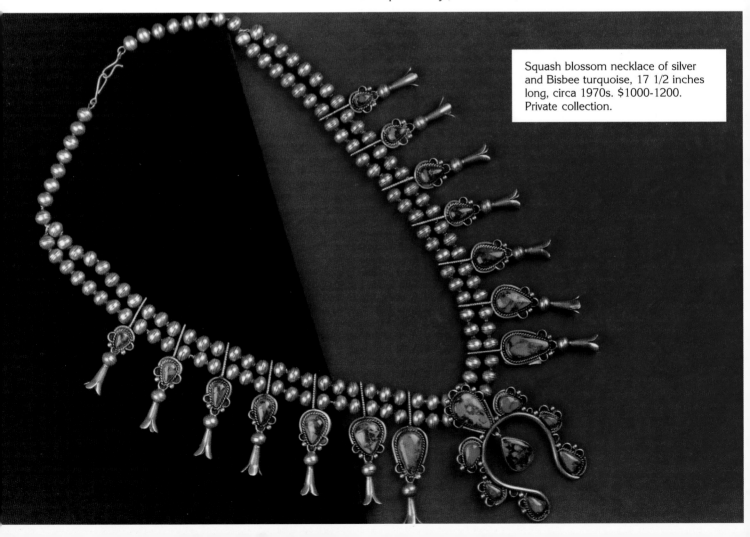

Squash blossom necklace of silver and Bisbee turquoise, 17 1/2 inches long, circa 1970s. $1000-1200. Private collection.

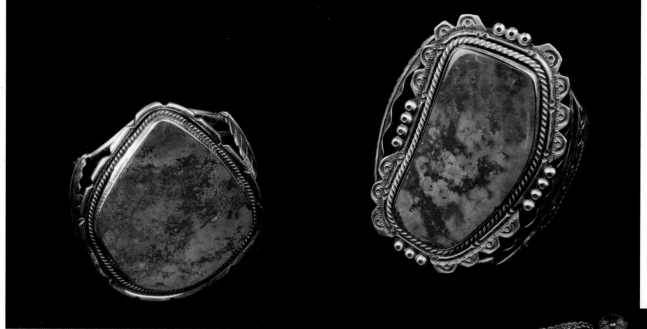

Two large silver cuff bracelets set with King turquoise from Colorado. $1000-1200 ea. Indian Post collection.

COLORADO

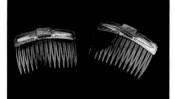

Hair ornaments. Pair of hair combs set with stablizied Manassa (Colorado) turquoise. Navajo, Courtesy of Palms Trading Company, Albuquerque. $65-80

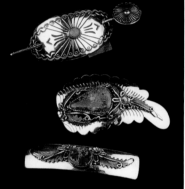

Large barrette set with natural Manassa (Colorado) turquoise by Peterson Johnson, Navajo, $165-190
Smaller barrette set with natural Manassa (Colorado) turquoise by Peterson Johnson, Navajo. $75-90
Pony tail pick and bar with turquoise set in sterling silver. Courtesy of Palms Trading Company, Albuquerque. $40-50

Necklace and earrings of silver and large oval stones of King Manassa turquoise, circa 1980s. $700-900. Indian Post collection.

Colorado turquoise mines include the **King** turquoise mine near **Manassa** which was rediscovered by I.P. King in 1890. The turquoise varies from light to sky-blue and a very attractive green with light brown matrix. The **Villa Grove** mine near LaJara was found about 1901 and has produced high quality hard turquoise of sky-to pale-blue with a brown or black matrix. Near the gold mines in Cripple Creek County, turquoise was found at the **Cripple Creek** mine. Soft turquoise suitable for treating was found in **Leadville** County.

There are a host of turquoise mines in Nevada, most found in the early years of the twentieth century, which have produced much of the turquoise stone found in the Indian-made jewelry. Strung through the mountains from north to south in the middle of the state, the turquoise mines fall into three general geographic areas.

In the northern **Battle Mountain** region of Nevada, the **Blue Gem** mine, also known as the **Turquoise Tunnel** and **Contention** mine, has been producing turquoise since 1934. Characteristically, Blue Gem turquoise has deep blue to deep green coloring in the same stone. Nearby, the **Lander Blue** mine is best known for its deep-to-light blue spider web turquoise with black matrix. The **No. 8** mine, operating in 1929, produced large nuggets of spider web in light to dark blue and green with brown and black matrix. The **Carlin** mine produced particularly hard, intense dark blue turquoise with a hard black matrix. The last three mines mentioned are all now closed. The **Stormy Mountain** mine has produced hard, light to dark blue turquoise with hard black matrix. The **Fox** mine, also called the **Cortez** mine, was discovered about 1910, and is one of the largest turquoise producers in the state. **Red Mountain** turquoise is known for its red and black-toned matrix. The **Carico Lake** mine, also known as the **Stone Cabin** mine, is the source for some of the turquoise with a knobby surface known as "seafoam." A recent mine is located at **Timberline** from which blue-green spider web turquoise is found. Quite nearby is the **Valley Blue** mine with mottled medium to dark blue turquoise in a red or black matrix or spider web figuring. In 1972, the **Darling/Darlene** mine was discovered in a mountainous area accessible only in the summer months. The turquoise here is light to deep blue or green.

NEVADA

Hidden Valley (Nevada) turquoise nugget. 6 lbs. 13 oz. 15,450 carats. Courtesy of Palms Trading Company, Albuquerque. $5,000

Belt with 438 carats of Lone Mountain (Nevada) turquoise clusters in sterling silver by D.S.J. Courtesy of Palms Trading Company, Albuquerque. $1,000-1200

Two pendants with natural oval Pilot Mountain (Nevada) turquoise of 142 carats set in sterling silver by Lonnie Willie, Navajo. Courtesy of Palms Trading Company, Albuquerque. $350-425

Leather ketoh with tufa cast sterling silver and No. 8 (Nevada) spiderweb turquoise by David Gaussoin, Picuris Pueblo and Navajo. Courtesy of David Gaussoin

Belt with tufa-cast sterling silver plaques set with Lone Mountain (Nevada) turquoise by Wayne Nez Gaussoin, Picuris Pueblo and Navajo. Courtesy of Wayne Nez Gaussoin

Royston turquoise set of squash blossom necklace with handmade beads, bracelet, ring, and earrings. Necklace is 31 3/4 inches long. $1800-2000. Private collection.

Near the center of Nevada around the town of Austin is the **Godber** mine, also known as the **Dry Creek, Burnham, Last Chance, Blue Stone** and **Homesite** mine, which was found about 1932. Its turquoise is hard and deep blue with a mottled black matrix sometimes going to a spider web figure. The **Zuni** mine is a smaller and recent turquoise producer of green to blue-green stone. The **McGinnis** mine, found in 1930, has also been called the **Gem** mine and produces turquoise of only fair quality. Both the **Blue Diamond** mine and the **Papoose** mine are at such high elevations that they can be worked only in the summer months. The Blue Diamond turquoise has characteristically been hard and mottled light to dark blue. The Papoose mine has produced deep blue stones with dark brown matrix and surface pits.

In the southern region of Nevada around the town of Tonopah are the third cluster of turquoise mines. The **Candeleria** mine has produced good quality turquoise. The **Ajax** mine is the source of a light blue stone with mottled green and dark blue patches. The **Montezuma** mine has yielded some hard, blue-green spider web stone, but the majority is soft. At the **Pilot** mine, turquoise of countless varieties have been found including green, blue and spider web stones with brown, black and mottled matrix. The **Smokey Valley** turquoise is usually light or medium blue. The **Royston** area's **Royal Blue** mine was discovered in 1902 and has given up stones of dark green and blue color with brown matrix. In 1920, the **Blue Jay** mine on Lone Mountain was found, but today the stone is referred to as **Lone Mountain** turquoise. Lone Mountain produces good to high quality turquoise of light to medium color. In 1907, the **Easter Blue** mine was discovered which produces light blue mottled spider web stones. The **Crow Springs** mine, which was found in 1909, is also known as the **Anjax** or **Bluebird** mine and is the source for pale to dark blue and green stones.

Sterling silver squash blossom necklace, earrings, and ring set with Stormy Mountain turquoise, circa 1970, with a tag reading, "Pawned for cash to buy a new pickup." $2200-2800. Dennehotso collection.

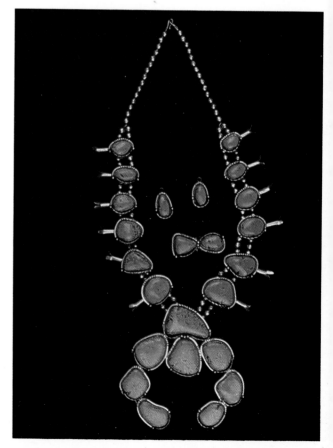

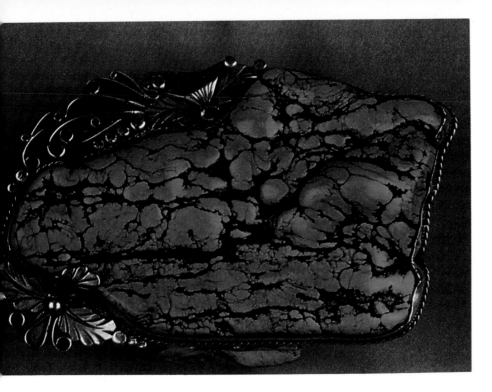

Extremely large ceremonial bracelet of silver set with one enormous Carico Lake turquoise stone, made by Johnson Platero, Navajo, 1980s. Turquoise Lady collection.

Silver bead stylized necklace with Zuni inlaid yei figures inlaid with Blue Gem turquoise by Rita Padilla, awarded the blue ribbon at the Gallup, N.M., Intertribal Indian Ceremonial in 1980. Private collection.

Squash blossom necklace with Smokey Mountain turquoise from northern Nevada, Navajo (Canoncito area), circa 1960s. $2000-2500. Maxwell Museum collection.

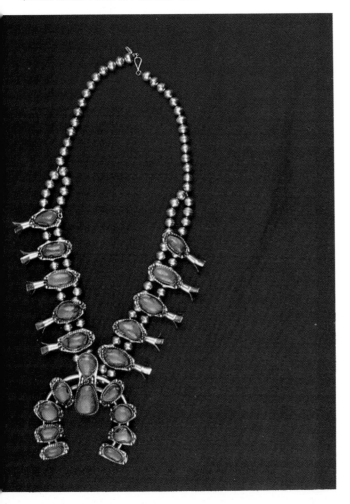

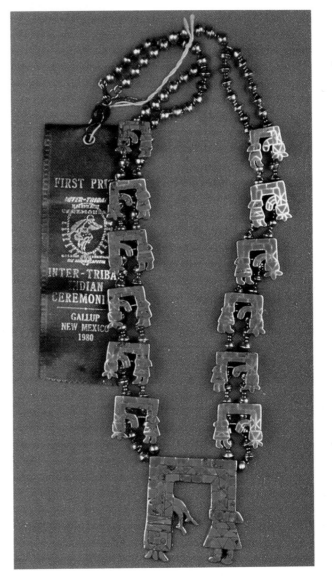

Outside of the United States, turquoise is found in a few isolated places including **Mexico, Peru, Chile** near the bauxite mines at Atacama, in **Australia, China** and **Tibet. Persian** turquoise, which since ancient times has been the world's standard of quality, is found in large quantity with clear blue color. Today, Persian producers send their turquoise to Germany for expert cutting and drilling.

FOREIGN

Bead and pendant necklace set with Tibetan turquoise and a cuff bracelet set with Chinese turquoise, both by Al Nez, Navajo, circa 1980s. $1800-2000. Indian Post collection.

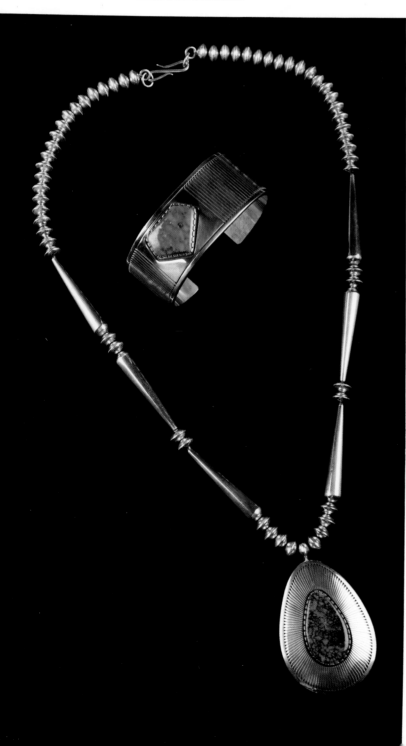

Persian turquoise, coral, and sterling silver necklace ornamented with inlaid, bird-designed plaques. $750-900. Maxwell Museum collection.

Mythology

Because it is a porous stone, turquoise appears darker when wet and lighter as it dries out, so that its changeable properties have caused turquoise to take on mystical significance to some groups.

Oriental tradition regards turquoise as able to reflect the health of its wearer. To them, as the color of turquoise paled, the owner sickened until death when the color was lost.[10] Arabian and Persian beliefs include the ability of turquoise to cure diseased heads and hearts. If taken orally alone or mixed with honey and other "drugs," they expected a cure from epilepsy. Taken with wine, it was expected to reverse the effects of poison and snake bite. Applied as an ointment to the eyes, it was believed to restore lost vision. Worn as an amulet, it insured happiness, drove away fear, and protected the wearer from drowning, lightning and snake bite. In Egypt, a cure for cataracts was claimed in "the local application of a turquoise set in a silver ring and dipped in water."[11]

In the arid American Southwest, different tribes attributed turquoise with various powers. Many associate it with water, and rain, because of both its color and texture variances when wet or dry. Pueblo tribes claim that turquoise stole its color from the sky. At Santo Domingo pueblo, turquoise is used for eyes on a prairie dog fetish of a rain god. At Zuni pueblo, where a perfect turquoise is male and an off color stone female, blue is the color of heaven, and indicates the western direction, because of blue twilight and the Pacific Ocean far to the west. Here a blue coyote fetish with turquoise eyes represents the West.[12]

The Navajo peoples learned of turquoise from the Pueblo tribes and incorporated turquoise into their evolving culture. Their beliefs have grown to include the power of turquoise to bring rain when it is thrown into a river with a prayer to the rain god. Because blowing wind is searching for the turquoise, an offering of turquoise to the wind will bring rain. With the Navajo, blue is associated with the South, and on Mount Taylor, the symbolic southern boundary marker, their super characters Turquoise Boy and Turquoise Girl live.[13]

Apache hunters attach a turquoise bead to a gun or bow to make it shoot accurately, and have often searched for turquoise at the end of a rainbow after a rain shower.

---

[10] Northrop, *Minerals*, p. 533.
[11] *Ibid*
[12] Pogue, *Turquois*, p. 124.
[13] *Ibid*, p. 125.

Wonderful bracelet with a four-part silver shank supporting a large No. 8 spider web turquoise stone. $400-550 / Three Navajo-made silver rings set with turquoise, shell, and pipestone. $75-120 ea. Turquoise Lady collection.

Fabulous quality Blue Gem and Morenci turquoise stones pump-drilled and strung as a necklace and jocla, circa 1915-20. $550-700. Crown & Eagle Antiques, Inc.

Jewelry Setting Techniques

American Indian jewelers are adept at setting and cutting turquoise. Many pieces of jewelry are designed to show off the beauty of the stone nugget itself. Often surrounded by wrought, filed and appliqued silver or gold, the turquoise can be the dominant decorative feature of the piece. Very often turquoise is cut as a cabochon with domed and polished surface to best expose its opaque luster.

Rough turquoise

Slabbed turquoise

Ground and sanded turquoise

Polished turquoise

Steps in cutting turquoise. Private collection.

TURQUOISE SET IN SILVER

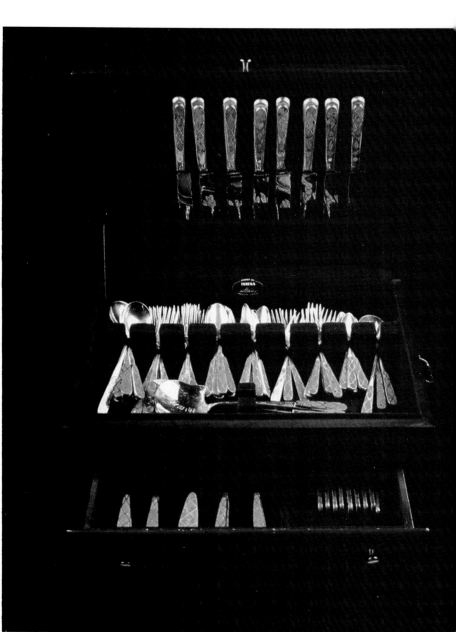

Full set of silver flatware ornamented with inlaid turquoise, made by Chee Yazzi, Navajo, in 1962. Private collection.

Cuff bracelet set with turquoise stones in a center row, made by Kee Benally, Navajo, circa 1970s. $250-300. Private collection.

Bracelet with 98 carat natural turquoise by Peterson Johnson, Navajo. Courtesy of Palms Trading Company, Albuquerque. $240-285

Buckle with black enamel border and turquoise. $200-250 / Silver and turquoise bow guard. $300-350 / Oval silver buckle with applique decoration and turquoise, made by Jerry White of Tuba City, Arizona. $250-300 / Zuni ranger style buckle on a black leather strap. $300-350 / Brown leather belt with turquoise-set buckle, made by V. Dishta, Zuni. $350-400. Leonard D. Prins collection.

Two shell ornaments for the corn dance with turquoise and mother of pearl mosaic decoration. Maxwell Museum collection.

Some turquoise is expertly cut into precise shapes to fit a predesigned silver wire frame, in a technique called "inlay," for the stone is actually laid into the wire frame. Small cut stones mounted together without the wire frames are referred to as "mosaics." Cut turquoise since ancient time has also been fashioned into animal and bird fetishes important to tribal culture as well as decorative. Turquoise beads drilled for stringing have been made since ancient times. Beads can be highly polished or finished to a matte surface.

Pendant inlaid with turquoise, shell, wood, and fossilized ivory by David Gaussoin, Picuris Pueblo and Navajo. Courtesy of David Gaussoin

INLAY

Inlay decorations ornament each of these bracelets, pins, rings, and one pair of earrings made at Zuni pueblo, circa 1930s-1940s. $250-300 ea. Lynn D. Trusdell collection.

Zuni silver and inlay bracelet and matching ring with white shell background and turquoise, coral and jet inlay, 1950s. $225-275 / Ring and pin with tortoise shell backgrounds and inlaid knifewing god figures, circa 1950. $200-225 / Two pins with black jet backgrounds and inlaid geometric design, circa 1950. $250-300. Enchanted Mesa collection.

Zuni-made inlay decorates a pair of drop earrings, a roadrunner pin, and a pin, ring, and earrings set all with tortoise shell. The turquoise and shell inlay on the matching set define the stylized design. $500-600. Enchanted Mesa collection.

Tortoise shell forms the backgrounds for each of these pieces at left, a bracelet with coral, shell, and turquoise inlay as a mudhead figure. $100-125 / Matching bracelet and ring with inlaid hano clown design. $250 / Pendant with standing kachina design. $100-125. Enchanted Mesa collection.

Zuni channel inlay group featuring turquoise set in silver on a link bracelet, oval buckle, earrings, and pins, circa 1950s. $700-900. Fred and Margarete Chase collection.

Group of five Zuni inlaid bracelets and a necklace featuring needlepoint stones in the border. All pieces circa 1930s-1940s. $1500-1800. Lynn D. Trusdell collection.

Sterling silver group featuring chip turquoise inlay: Necklace with water birds accented with coral. / Bracelet made by S.D. / Buckle with bird design made by the Dodge family. All pieces circa 1980s. $700-900. Leonard D. Prins collection.

Silver bracelet, ring and pendant inlaid with turquoise and lapis lazuli, made by Andy Kirk, Navajo, 1980s. $800-900

Turquoise, silver, shell, and lapis lazuli inlaid pendant with silver chain, and an inlaid coral and lapis bracelet, all made by Ray Tracey, Navajo, circa 1980s. $300-350. Indian Post collection.

PETIT POINT AND NEEDLEPOINT

Zuni silver chain and turquoise necklace. $225 / Large bracelet of turquoise inlaid in silver. $150-195 / Small bracelet and two rings of needlepoint turquoise circa 1980s. $350-425 Indian Post collection.

Turquoise cut to uniform size with one end rounded and the other end pointed is known as "petit point." When the turquoise is cut with two pointed ends it is known as "needlepoint." Small round domed pieces of turquoise are sometimes called "snake eyes."

Necklace of three round medallions and matching earrings made by Seowaqseow, circa 1960s. $250-300 / Hoop earrings with fringe turquoise. $65-95 pr. / Fringe necklace with turquoise made by L.W. $300-400. Private collection.

Squash blossom necklace set with turquoise, made by Willie Yazzie, Jr., Navajo. $600-800 / Bracelet with clustered turquoise. $300-400 / Big round pin with petit point turquoise, made by F.M. Begay, Navajo, circa 1980s. $250-300. Leonard D. Prins collection.

Jewelry Forms —

BEAD NECKLACES

Turquoise chunks are featured in this bead necklace with shell heishe closure string. $250-275 / Cuff bracelet of wrought silver. $95-130 / Finger ring, circa 1980s. $35-50. Leonard D. Prins collection.

Three turquoise bead necklaces, circa 1980s: At left, small necklace of chunks of Lone Mountain turquoise. $100-125 / Zuni bear fetishes are graduated and strung with turquoise beads. $400-450 / Six strands of natural turquoise beads. $700-1000. Leonard D. Prins collection.

From the top: Three strands of turquoise nuggets and shell heishe form a necklace, 1976. $95-120 / Large nuggets of Tuscarara turquoise in a single strand necklace, 1977. $300-350 / Gold beads and pendant of Lone Mountain turquoise, circa 1970s-1980s. $95-125 / Small nuggets of Lone Mountain turquoise, 1976. $60-80. Private collection.

Thirty-strand turquoise heishe necklace from the Santo Domingo pueblo, circa 1980s. $800-1000

Heishe of olivella shell dating from the 1940s and turquoise beads form a five-string necklace by Mary Aguilar, Santo Domingo, 1969. Maxwell Museum collection.

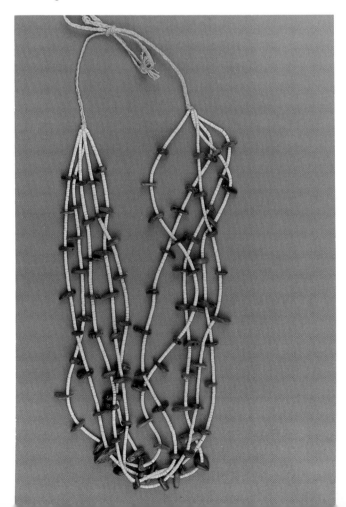

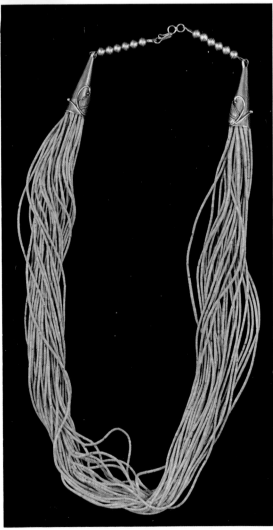

25

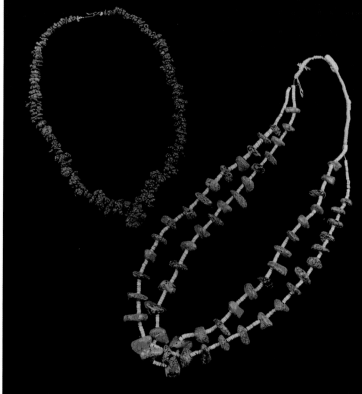

Choker of graduated Lone Mountain turquoise chunks. $350-400 /
Two-strand necklace of white shell heishe and turquoise. $480-600.
Private collection on permanent loan to Ohio University.

A four-strand shell and turquoise bead necklace with a
pair of joclas with coral made by Marietta Wetherill, circa
1950s. $1350-1500. Maxwell Museum collection.

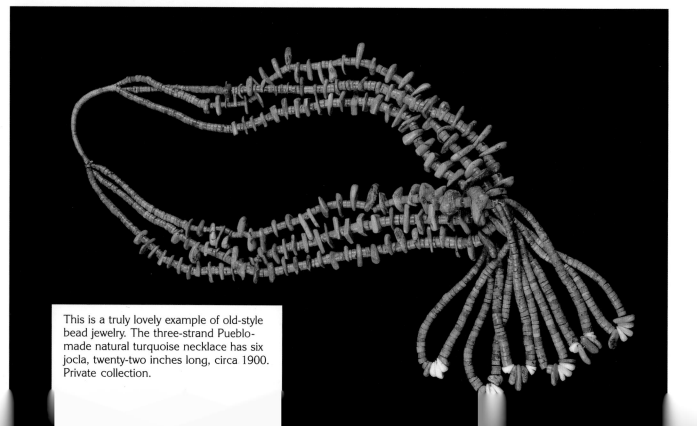

This is a truly lovely example of old-style
bead jewelry. The three-strand Pueblo-
made natural turquoise necklace has six
jocla, twenty-two inches long, circa 1900.
Private collection.

A wrought silver and turquoise "marriage crown". A marvelous heavy necklace with large turquoise chunks. $400-500. Leonard D. Prins collection.

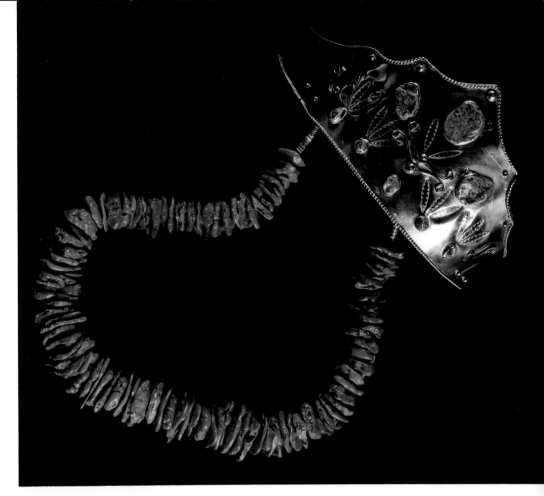

Extravagant three-strand necklace with turquoise "bear claws," made with stabilized Kingman mine turquoise, disc-cut beads and sterling silver, circa 1970. $1000-1200. Dennehotso collection.

Bear paw-shaped turquoise beads strung as a necklace, 23 1/2 inches long, 1976. $1000-1200. Private collection.

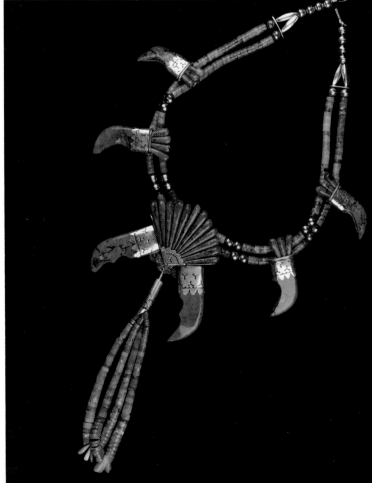

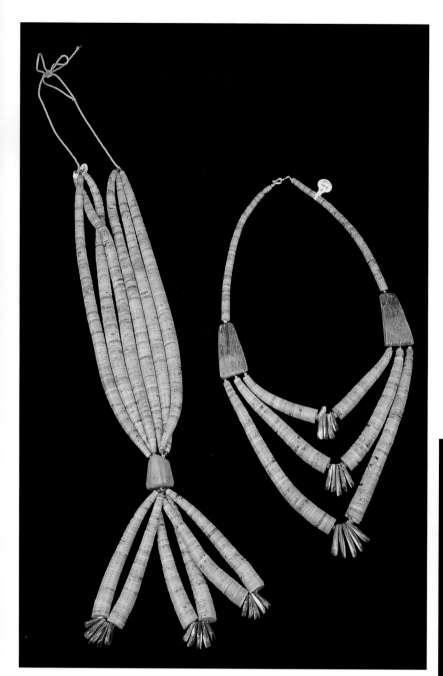

Fetish necklace with assorted stone birds, including turquoise. Courtesy of Palms Trading Company, Albuquerque. $150-200

Turquoise three-strand bead necklace with jacla by Lupe Levato. Santo Domingo. $1200-1500
Turquoise bead necklace with coral by Lupe Levato, Santo Domingo. Courtesy of Palms Trading Company, Albuquerque. $450-550

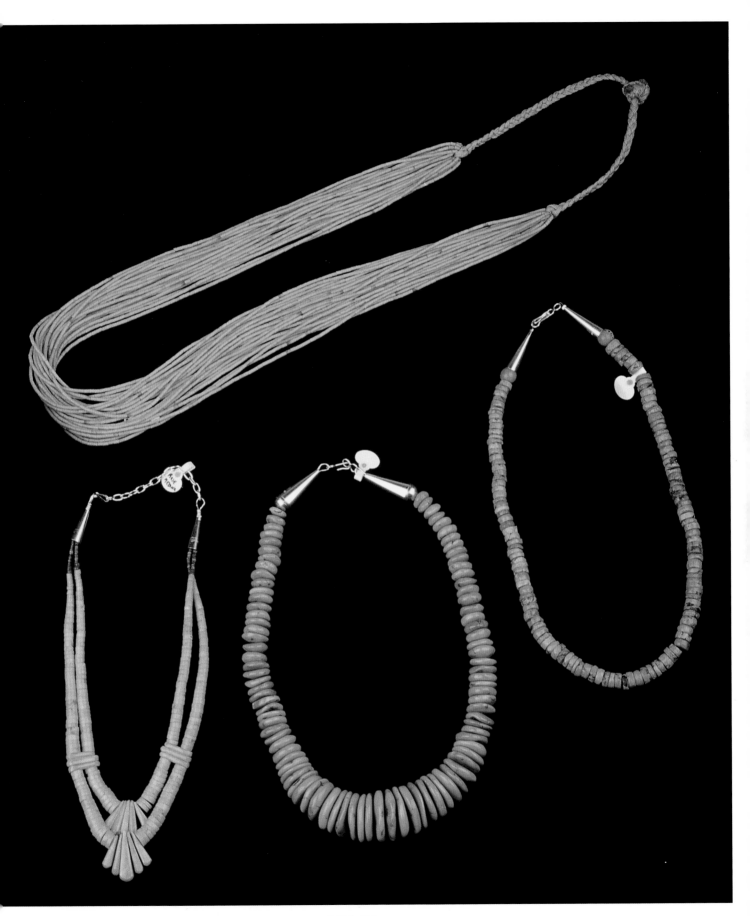

25-strand turquoise heishi necklace by Luciano Bailow. $700-800
2-strand turquoise choker with drops by Rose Medina. $375-450
Single strand green turquoise bead necklace. $235-325
Single strand graduate and turquoise bead necklace. Courtesy of Palms Trading Company, Albuquerque. $135-150

BRACELETS

Wrought and stamped silver bracelet with a large square turquoise stone. $600-800. Maxwell Museum collection.

Two silver hand-wrought cuff bracelets, the smaller stone is colored porcelain, both circa 1910. $500-800. Enchanted Mesa collection.

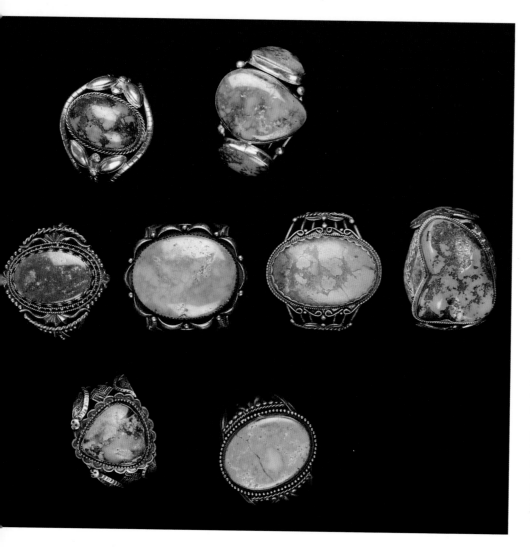

Bracelet with enhanced turquoise set in sterling silver. Courtesy of Palms Trading Company, Albuquerque. $130-175

Eight bracelets with strong personalities: (Top row): Oval Bisbee egg-shaped stone, circa 1950s / Three irregular Royston turquoise stones on round wire, circa 1960s / (Center row): Elaborate silver work and fabulous quality turquoise stone, circa 1920 / Easter blue turquoise, circa 1950s / Cerillos turquoise with stamped serrated bezel, circa 1915-1920 / Irregular and heavy Morenci turquoise stone, circa 1940s / (Bottom row): Cerillos turquoise with snakes criss-crossing and log stamp on each side, circa 1930s / Large Easter blue turquoise stone, circa 1930s. $600-800 ea. Lynn D. Trusdell collection.

Silver bracelet with three old turquoise stones from different mines: left, a Morenci turquoise stone; center, a Cerillos turquoise which was previously drilled as an ear bob; right, a Blue Gem turquoise stone. $800-1200. Lynn D. Trusdell collection.

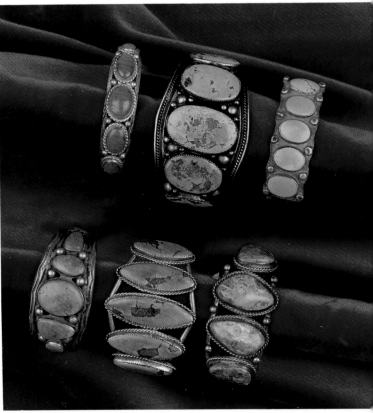

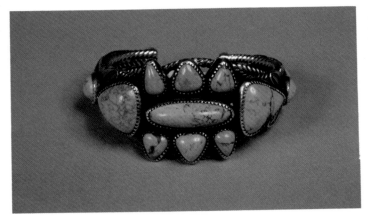

Zuni silver cluster bracelet of wonderful quality. $450-500. Lynn D. Trusdell collection.

Six sterling silver Navajo bracelets, featuring: Morenci turquoise, circa 1950 / Villa Grove turquoise, circa 1950 / Carlin, Nevada, turquoise, circa 1950 / Low-end Castle Dome turquoise with handmade die stamps and hand-rolled sterling silver, circa 1915 / Slagpile Bisbee turquoise, circa 1965 / Royston, Nevada, turquoise, circa 1965. $450-700 ea. Dennehotso collection.

Three silver cuff bracelets of good quality set with turquoise. $250-400 ea. Lynn D. Trusdell collection.

Three sand-cast silver bracelets, two with turquoise inlay, Navajo-Window-rock. $195-300 ea. Enchanted Mesa collection.

Navajo silver bracelet set with turquoise. $300-400. Lynn D. Trusdell collection.

Five Navajo silver bracelets: From top, large bracelet with coral branch and numerous turquoise stones. / Two large Bisbee turquoise nuggets. / Bouquet of turquoise nuggets. / Oval turquoise and coral stones. / Eight turquoise stones with one large in the center. $300-450 ea. Private collection.

Three Navajo silver bow guards: left, circa 1915-1920. / Center, a sand cast silver bow guard, circa 1930s. / Right, circa 1920s. $400-500 ea. Lynn D. Trusdell collection.

Two sterling silver cuff bracelets: four rows of turquoise by Paul Stungaten, $1,000-1200
Bear claw; coral, and turquoise bracelet by M. Tsosie, $275-325
Courtesy of Palms Trading Company, Albuquerque.

Tufa-cast sterling silver bracelet with turquoise set in a 14 carat gold bezel, and coral beads by Connie Tsosie Gaussoin, Picuris Pueblo and Navajo. Courtesy of Connie Tsosie Gaussoin

Line bracelet set with needlepoint turquoise, made by Douglas Lesence, circa 1940s. $250-300. Maxwell Museum collection.

Bracelet of wrought and stamped silver with three rows of round turquoise stones. $300-400. Adobe Gallery collection.

3-line bracelet with round turquoise stones. $175-250

Five Zuni sterling silver bracelets with three rows of turquoise each, including: Morenci turquoise / "Snake Eye" Kingman turquoise / Turquoise from various mines, made from 1920s to 1950s. $250-400 ea. Dennehotso collection.

Navajo bracelet set with turquoise. $400-600. Lynn D. Trusdell collection.

Child's Zuni cluster bracelet, circa 1945. $400-500. Maxwell Museum collection.

Turquoise cluster bracelet of silver probably made by a non-Indian, circa 1970s. $500-700. Lynn D. Trusdell collection.

Silver bracelet set with a cluster of turquoise stones. $450-550. Lynn D. Trusdell collection.

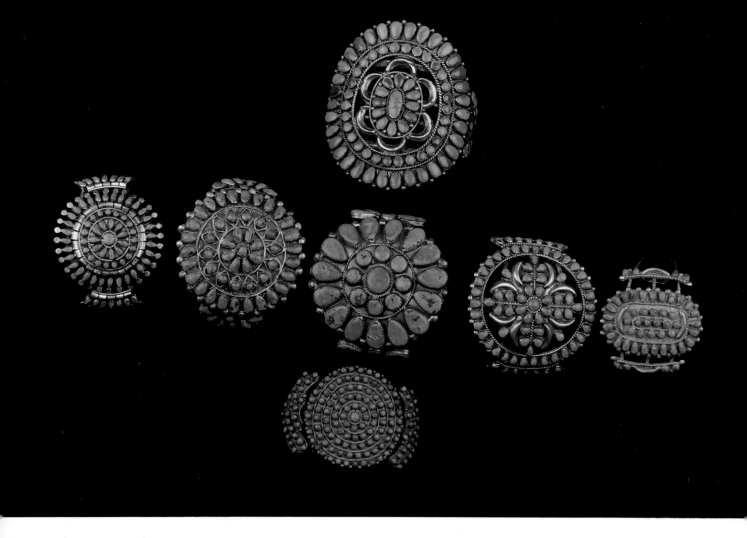

Seven Zuni cluster bracelets set with: Morenci turquoise, circa 1950. / Lone Mountain turquoise, circa 1950. / Smokey Valley, Nevada, turquoise, circa 1950. $250-400 ea. Dennehotso collection.

Stunning petit point bracelet by Bonnie Quam and Pete Gonzalez, Zuni, 1960. $400-500. Maxwell Museum collection.

Matching bracelet and ring in silver with cut-out heart design and needlepoint turquoise inlay. $125-150. Indian Traders West collection.

Group of finely made Zuni silver bracelets set in channel inlay with light colored turquoise. $225-275 ea. Enchanted Mesa collection.

Zuni silver bracelet with turquoise channel inlay. $250-300. Private collection.

Silver bangle bracelet and ring channel inlaid with yellow mother of pearl and turquoise, made by J.B. Zuni. / Bracelet and ring of silver with turquoise channel inlay, made by E. C. Seoutewa, Zuni. / Bangle bracelet set with six rows of five columns of turquoise channel inlay, made by C.H. and P. K. H., Zuni. / Bracelet and matching ring of turquoise channel inlay, made by E. C. Seoutewa, Zuni. Bracelets, $150-200 ea.; Rings, $100-125 ea. Leonard D. Prins collection.

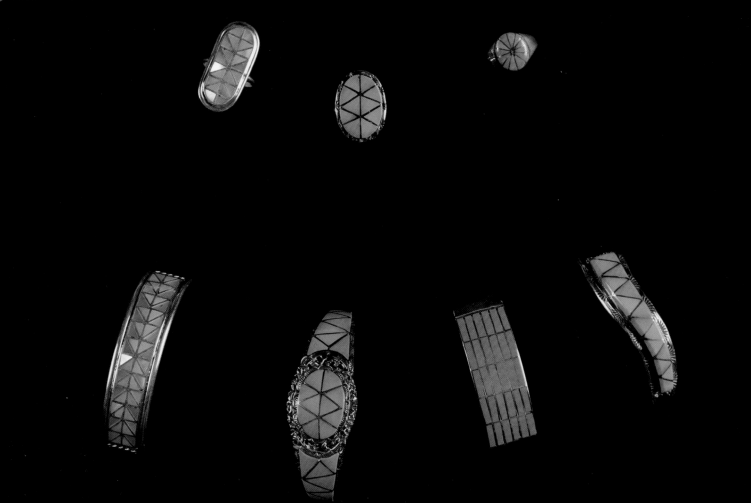

Two silver bracelets by Gibson Nez, circa 1980s: Wide silver band with round Chinese turquoise stone / Bisbee turquoise in cut-out silver band. $250-300 ea. Indian Post collection.

Four Navajo silver bracelets with stone to stone inlay made by A.B. / Zuni silver bracelet inlaid with bird designs, made by B.H. $200-300 ea. Leonard D. Prins collection.

Two cuff bracelets of 18 k. gold plating on silver with applique work and turquoise, shell, jet and coral accents, unmarked. Jim Silva collection.

RINGS, PINS, AND EARRINGS

Needlepoint turquoise and silver cross made by Rosemary Panteah, Zuni, circa 1980s. / Round cluster pendant, 1976. / Snowflake pin with 188 Morenci turquoise needlepoint stones, Zuni, circa 1965. / Round pendant by Rosemary Panteah, Zuni. $150-300 ea. Private collection.

Two Zuni finger rings set with channel inlay turquoise. Smaller one by W. Lacco, $85-120 Larger one by DEB. Courtesy of Palms Trading Company, Albuquerque. $85-120

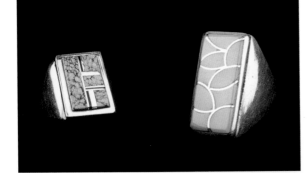

Nine old Navajo pins of silver set with turquoise, featuring: Morenci turquoise, made by Victor M. Begay, Navajo, circa 1950s / One from a set of five, Zuni, circa 1950 / Blouse pin made of Morenci turquoise, from a set of ten, circa 1950. / Kingman turquoise, circa 1960. / Morenci needlepoint turquoise by Victor M. Begay, Navajo, circa 1950s. / Kingman turquoise, circa 1960. Morenci turquoise, circa 1930s. / Small cluster of Morenci turquoise, circa 1940s. Small pins, $35-50 ea.; Large pins, $150-250 ea. Dennehotso collection.

Four pairs of turquoise earrings, including: Nugget dangles / Single nuggets /
Zuni dangles / Ring dangles. $95-175 pr. Private collection.

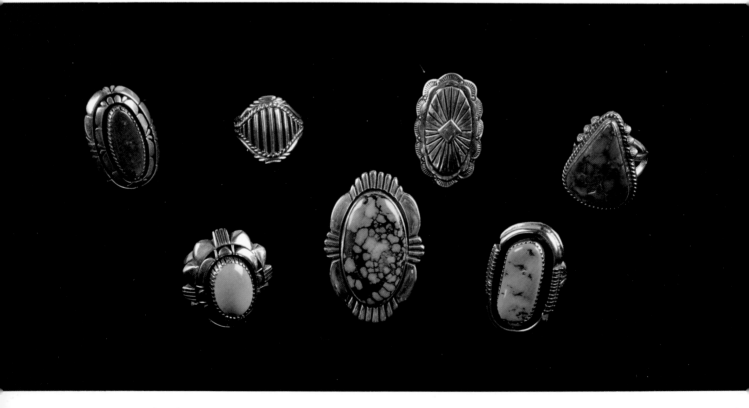

Group of Navajo lady's rings of turquoise and silver. $50-150 ea.
Leonard D. Prins collection.

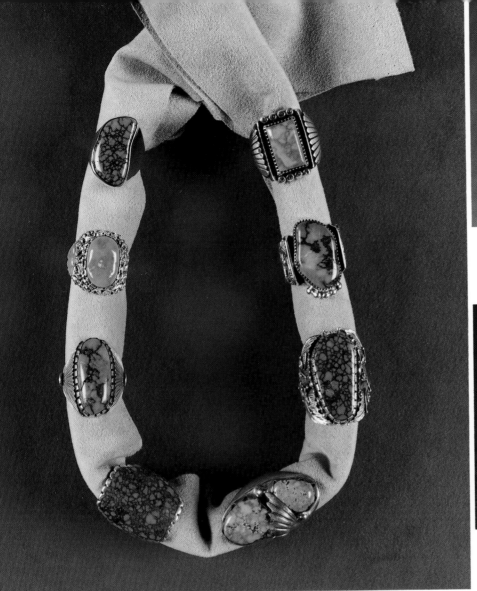

Zuni silver ring set with oval and petite point turquoise stones. $200-300. Adobe Gallery collection.

Navajo silver ring with stamped design and set with turquoise. $150-225. Adobe Gallery collection.

Eight silver rings, including: Long oval Indian Mountain turquoise with grey matrix by Tsosie, Navajo, 1976. / Bisbee turquoise with five balls at the top and cast side figures, 1982. / Cast silver with oval nuggets and three inlays on one side by Lee and Mary Weebothee, Zuni, 1989. / Rectangular stone, 1988. / Ovoid stone in leaf cast setting of Indian Mountain turquoise by Boyd Tsosie, Navajo. / Two nuggets of Morenci turquoise, 1976. / Plain setting with kidney-shaped Lone Mountain turquoise. / Curved Lone Mountain spider web turquoise by Lee Yazzie, Navajo, 1980. $125-225 ea. Private collection on permanent loan to Ohio University.

Two pins with clustered turquoise set in silver: the larger one Navajo, the smaller one Zuni, circa 1930s. $150-200 ea. Lynn D. Trusdell collection.

Early Navajo ring of silver with turquoise stones. $250-300. Adobe Gallery collection.

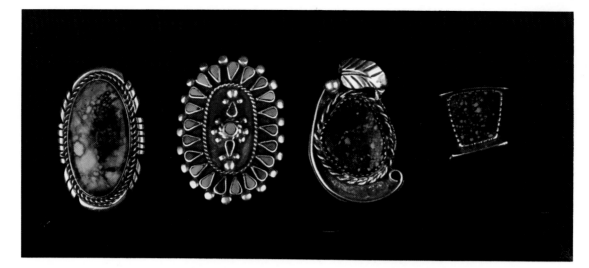

Ring with split sterling silver shank and oval turquoise stone. / Petit point cluster turquoise ring with two wire shanks. / Ring with silver decorated frame and turquoise. / Ring with Landers Blue turquoise and fourteen-carat gold. $95-225 ea. Turquoise Lady collection.

Seven Zuni pins set with turquoise, including: Large round pin by Y. and R. Charley. / three turquoise stones set in silver by J.R.D. / Large, four-sided turquoise stone set by a member of the Platero family. / Other pins unmarked. $75-300 ea. Indian Post collection.

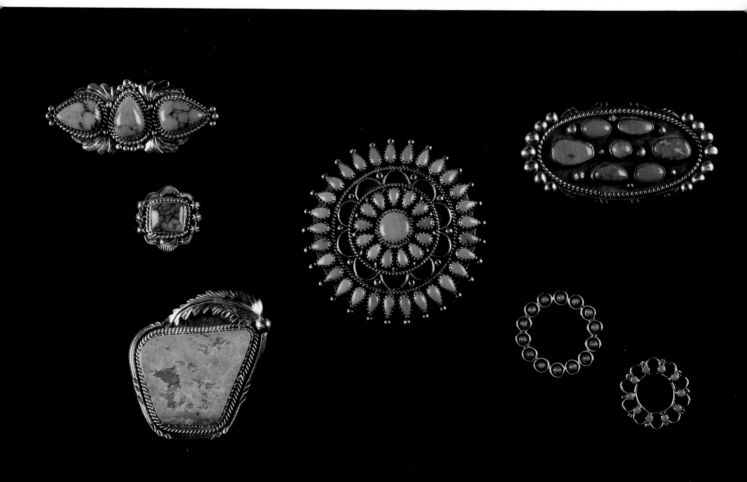

Group of eight rings of silver set with turquoise: the larger stoned rings are Navajo-made: three are Zuni-made, circa 1920s - 1940s. $125-225 ea. Lynn D. Trusdell collection.

Zuni turquoise channel inlay group including two pins and two pairs of earrings in swirl designs by Quandelacy. $70-145 pr. Enchanted Mesa collection.

Group of Zuni pendants, rings, and a stick pin circa 1970s: From top: pendant with tortoise shell background by T. Ohmsatte. / Mickey Mouse ring of inlay. / Flower pendant with turquoise inlay by C. and K. / Mickey Mouse stick pin by B.P. / Owl inlay ring / Snoopy inlay ring / Flower pendant with coral center by S. Leekya. $75-125 ea. Turquoise Lady collection.

Two turquoise and silver ring and earrings sets by Albert Platero,
Navajo, circa 1980s. $200-300 set. Private collection.

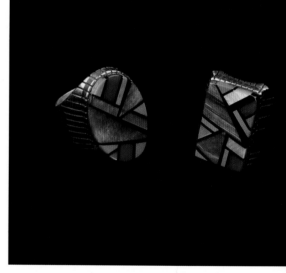

Two Zuni inlay man's rings, circa late 1980s.
$125-175 ea. Indian Post collection.

Seven Zuni rings of silver with stone inlay of figural and geometric
designs, 1989. $95-125 ea. Bing Crosby collection.

Three pair of earrings: Zuni needlepoint
turquoise, $90-110
Zuni drop style with turquoise bead. $165-190
Navajo with enhanced Turquoise Mountain
turquoise. Courtesy of Palms Trading
Company, Albuquerque. $100-125

BELTS

Three old Navajo concha belts set with turquoise: A third phase concha belt with Cerillos turquoise, circa 1910. / Clusters of Blue Gem turquoise on original leather, circa 1920. / Linked large conchas, circa 1930s. Lynn D. Trusdell collection.

Group of man's ranger belts, circa 1970s, including: Black leather with channel inlay buckle made by L.M., Zuni. / Chisel work buckle with Persian turquoise made by C. Johnson, 1976. / No. 8 turquoise on buckle made for Tobe Turpen (shop mark). $300-400 ea. Private collection.

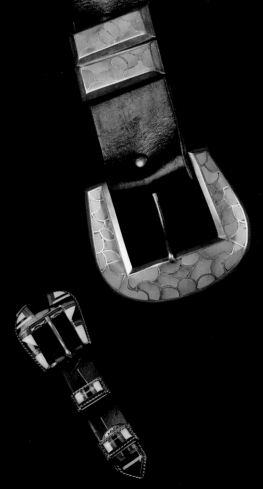

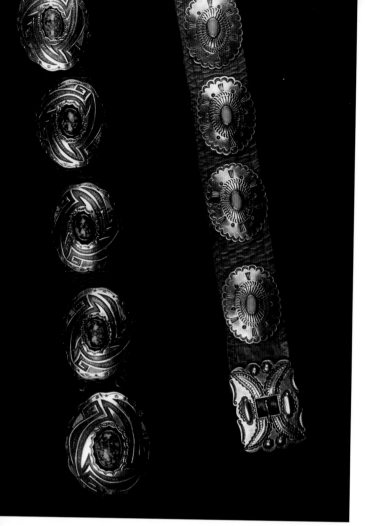

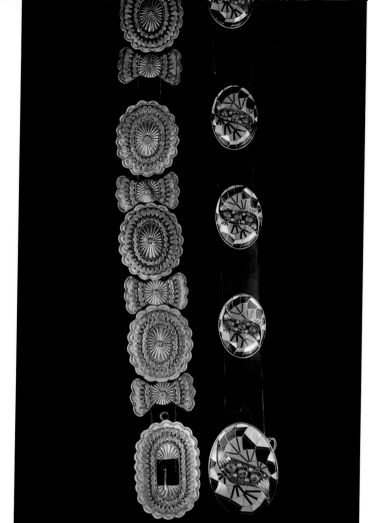

Two silver concha belts, circa 1980s, featuring Persian turquoise on the black belt. / Czechoslovakian glass centers on the brown belt with eleven conchas. Private collection.

Two handsome silver concha belts, one set with turquoise channel inlay leaves. / The other set with petit point turquoise stones. Private collection.

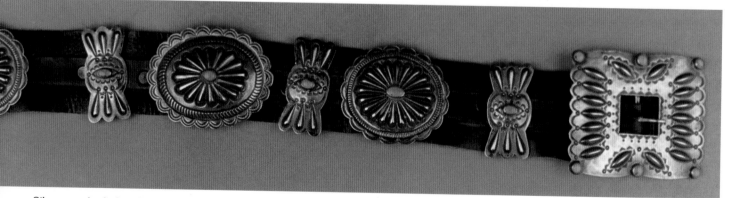

Silver concha belt with turquoise accents, circa 1920s-1930s. Maxwell Museum collection.

Opposite:
Six concha belts, including nickel belt, machine stamped with buckle and ten conchas, circa 1960s. / Sterling silver with eighteen-gauge silver, buckle, seven stamped conchas and eight butterflies, Navajo, circa 1950s. / Six conchas, buckle, seven butterflies, eighteen-gauge sterling silver, fifteen Morenci and Villa grove turquoise stones, Navajo, circa 1900. Unusual butterfly design probably copied from Spanish-Mexican head stall piece. / Buckle, six conchas, four butterflies, eighteen-gauge sterling silver, fine stamping dies, Navajo, circa early 1900s. / Buckle, seven conchas, six butterflies, eleven Morenci turquoise stones, Navajo, circa 1900. / Buckle, seven conchas, six butterflies, twenty-gauge sterling silver, Navajo, circa 1920s. Dennehotso collection.

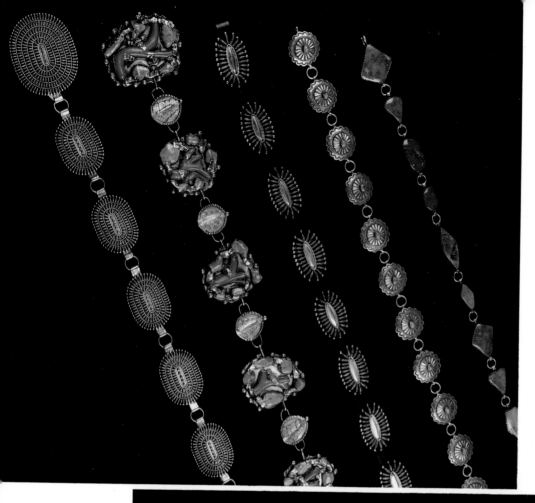

Five lady's concha belts, each set with turquoise, circa 1970s-1980s: From the left, petit point turquoise link belt by Rosemary Panteah, Zuni. / Seven conchas and eight butterflies of coral and Nevada blue turquoise by Wayne Calavaza, Zuni, 1933. / Needlepoint turquoise with fourteen conchas and buckle (each concha has twenty-four stones). / Linked silver medallions with turquoise centers. / Linked chunks of turquoise. $300-450 ea. Private collection.

Three silver belts, circa 1980s: From left, large silver conchas and a buckle with six turquoise pieces. Brown leather with openwork sand-cast medallions and turquoise accents. / Black leather with small silver coins and turquoise in the centers. $750-1000 ea. Leonard D. Prins collection.

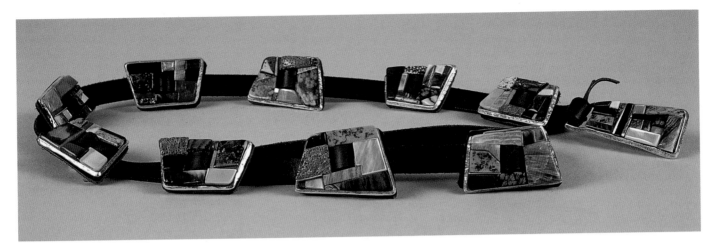

"Painted Desert" concha belt of tufa cast sterling silver plaques inlaid with various natural turquoise, onyx, mother of pearl, coral and shell by David Gaussoin, Picuris Pueblo and Navajo. In the collection of the Heard Museum, Phoenix, Arizona. Courtesy of David Gaussoin

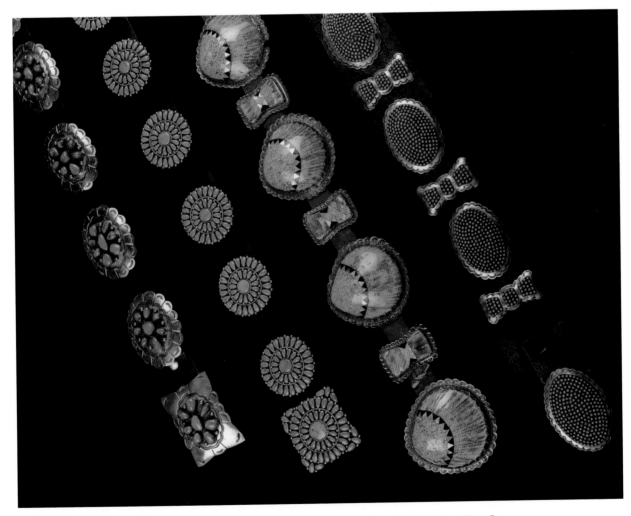

Four stunning belts, circa 1970s. From left, turquoise and silver conchas with sixty-four Blue Gem turquoise nuggets by P.H.Y. / Round medallions with thirty-nine petit points and one round turquoise stone in each cluster (366 stones total) by Alice Quam, Zuni. Forty-nine inches long. / Turquoise, jet, shell, and mother of pearl on five spiny oyster shells with silver bezels around the edges and Indian Mountain turquoise with a brown/gold matrix made by Cheryl Marie Yescerva. / Seven silver conchas and eight spacers set with 2400 round turquoise stones made by Harold Gray. Private collection.

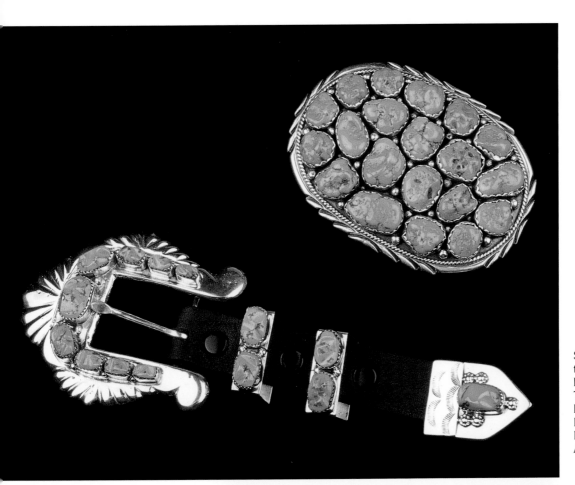

Sterling silver and turquoise nugget buckle by C. Yazzi. $400-450 Turquoise nugget ranger buckle set by T. & L. Leekity, Zuni. Courtesy of Palms Trading Company, Albuquerque. $285-325.

Seven silver buckles: From left, oval with spider web turquoise by Gibson Nez, Navajo, 1979. / Small oval, all silver, unmarked. / Rectangular buckle with three rows of turquoise, made by M.F.C., 1982. / Needlepoint oval buckle made by V.M.B., 1976. / Oval buckle with eleven Kingman nuggets, made by Bitsui and Russell, 1982. / Oval buckle with eleven Kingman nuggets, made by Bitsui and Russell, 1982. / Oval buckle with center piece and a row of turquoise, made by W.M., 1988. / Turquoise and coral buckle made for Tobe Turpen (shop mark). $150-400 ea. Private collection.

Opposite:
Six silver belt buckles, circa 1980s: Top row, eagle inlay with turquoise, coral, and tortoise shell by R.N.L., Zuni. / King Manassa stones in silver with applique by J.P. / Large turquoise stone in silver made by Robert Lee Bya. / A small turquoise stone and silver made by Ned Nez. / Rectangular silver buckle with a small triangular turquoise stone, made by Joseph H. Quintana, Cochiti. / Four turquoise stones set in silver, made by Dan Simplicio, Zuni. $300-400 ea. Indian Post collection.

Five sterling silver buckles made circa 1989: From top, oval with turquoise, coral, and bear claw made by E. / Oval stone inlay design made by W.V. Quam, Zuni. / Rectangular buckle with inlaid fire and dancing figure by B.B. / Small oval inlay buckle of geometric stone design. / Rectangular stone mosaic design by E. Ohmsatte. $175-250 ea. Bing Crosby collection.

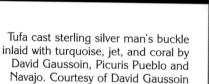

Tufa cast sterling silver man's buckle inlaid with turquoise, jet, and coral by David Gaussoin, Picuris Pueblo and Navajo. Courtesy of David Gaussoin

Four sand-cast silver Navajo buckles each set with a turquoise stone. $150-200 ea. Enchanted Mesa collection.

Matching necklace and bracelet of silver set with Kingman turquoise and branch coral, circa 1970s. $500-600 / Pendant necklace of silver beads with round and melon-shaped beads, Carlin turquoise, and coral, circa 1970. $250-350 / Bead necklace with Bisbee turquoise and coral, circa 1970. $250-300. Dennehotso collection.

SILVER NECKLACES

Three pendants, including a silver bead necklace and pendant with five coral pieces on each side of a turquoise stone, 20 3/4 inches long, by Gibson Nez, Navajo. / Triangular green Nevada turquoise stone pendant set in silver by Lee Edaakie. / Oval turquoise and silver pendant on a silver chain. Private collection.

Silver bead necklace with six turquoise stones by V. and R. Charley. $550-800 / Silver cuff bracelet with turquoise made by Lolli Willeta. $350-450. Leonard D. Prins collection.

Stone-and-shell-inlaid sterling silver link necklace by Sue Ellen Kalestewa, Zuni, 1989. $125-175 / Bear fetish sterling silver and turquoise bead necklace by Clifton Hamone, 1989. $65-80. Bing Crosby collection.

Squash blossom necklace with thirteen turquoise stones and twelve stones in the naja, made by Chee, circa 1940s-1950s. $800-950. Lynn D. Trusdell collection.

Petit point turquoise squash blossom necklace and earrings set by Rosemary Panteah, Zuni, 1976. Necklace has twelve blossoms, each with sixty-six stones. Naja has 112 stones. More than 800 stones total and measures 28 3/4 inches long. $1000-1200. Private collection.

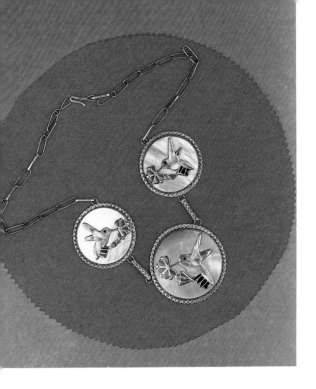

Hummingbird inlay on round shell medallions forming a link necklace with silver chain, Zuni. $400-450. Enchanted Mesa collection.

Squash blossom necklace with silver beads and petit point turquoise, Zuni, circa 1950. $400-500 / Necklace of silver links set with turquoise, made by Lee Yazzie, Navajo, circa 1980. $200-250. Indian Post collection.

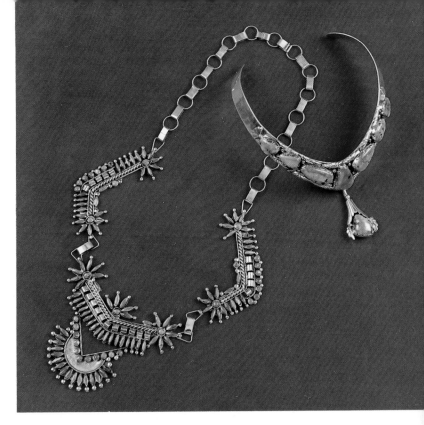

Two silver chokers set with turquoise: left, link-style necklace with needlepoint turquoise, made by Valentino and Matilda Banteah, Zuni, in 1975. $450-500 / Right, a fixed silver choker and pendant set with seven turquoise stones, made for Tobe Turpin (shop mark), circa 1970s. $300-450. Private collection on permanent loan to Ohio University.

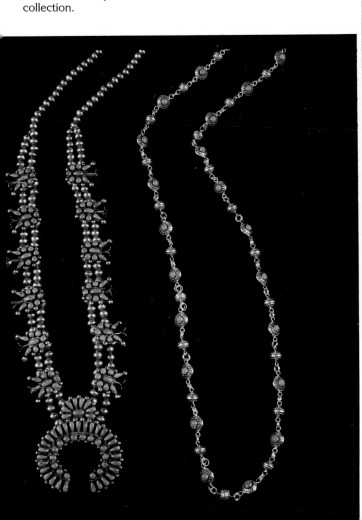

Silver Navajo squash blossom necklace and matching earrings with a turquoise drop in the naja. $700-800. Enchanted Mesa collection.

Squash blossom necklace and earrings, Zuni. Courtesy of Palms Trading Company, Albuquerque. $435-500

Silver link necklace with large turquoise stones from Nevada set by Harry Jake. Navajo. $300-400. Indian Post collection.

BOLO TIES

Three Zuni bolo ties, $150-200 ea., and one buckle of silver decorated with turquoise, $350. Private collection.

Four bolo ties with slides and tips decorated with turquoise and silver, unmarked. $150-200 ea. Private collection.

Three Zuni bolo ties with multicolored geometric inlay by Albert Platero, Navajo, 1989. $175-225 ea. Bing Crosby collection.

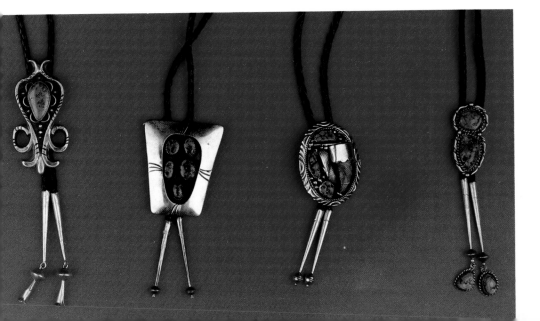

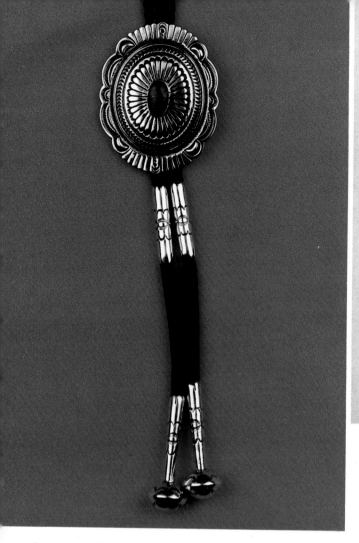

Bolo tie and tips of stamped silver and turquoise, made by Thomas Jim of Rocking Horse Ranch, Phoenix, Arizona. $150-225

At left, bolo slide of silver decorated with branch coral and two turquoise stones, made by David Benally, Navajo, 1976. / Rectangular silver plate with spear point and six turquoise stones, made by Stover Paul, Shiprock, New Mexico, 1975. $200-300 ea. Private collection on permanent loan to Ohio University.

Nickel silver bolo tie slide designed as a dancer with shell and stone inlay. $300-400. Turquoise Lady collection.

Old two-piece bolo set with bolo slide and buckle made from older bracelets. $500-600. Private collection on permanent loan to Ohio University.

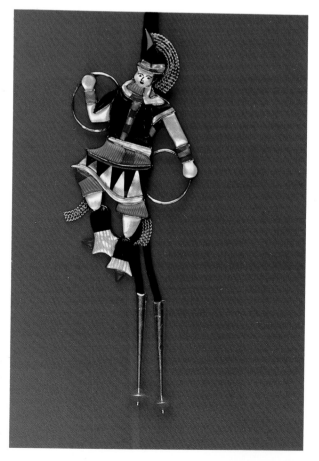

Navajo bolo tie slide of a silver Kachina dancer, circa 1950s. / Large turquoise stone set in appliqued silver, circa 1960s. $200-300. Crown & Eagle Antiques Inc. collection.

Three bolo ties, including: A cluster bolo and buckle set of No. 8 turquoise from Tobe Turpen (shop mark), 1980. / Triangular Kingman spider web turquoise stone by Mike Shirley, circa 1978. / Large turquoise nugget set by Lee Edaakie. $200-400 ea. Private collection.

Sunface designed inlaid bolo set with bolo tie, buckle, and cufflinks, made by AZ 3AP-TP. $450-500 set. Private collection.

MATCHING SETS

Sterling silver and turquoise necklace, bracelet, earrings, and ring set made by C. Jake, 1980s. $700-900. Leonard D. Prins collection.

Set featuring Number 8 turquoise, including: a squash blossom necklace with large naja, a bracelet, earrings, and a ring. Necklace is 30 5/8 inches long, made circa 1978. $800-1000. Private collection.

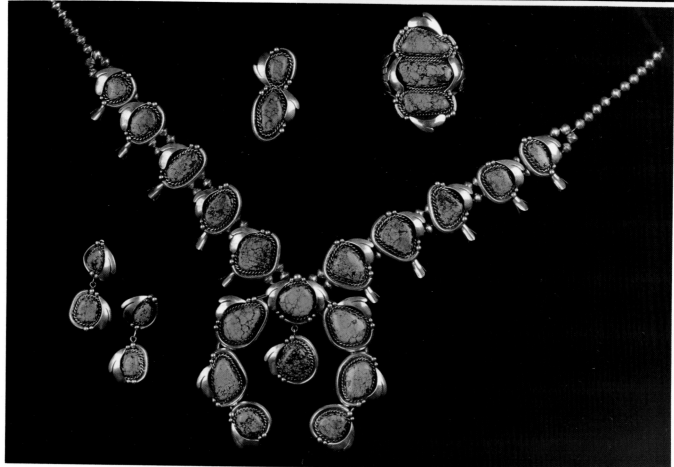

Necklace, bracelet and earrings of various beads including turquoise, white and glass trade beads, lapis lazuli, and Zuni stone fetishes, assembled by Flora Tenorio for Peyote Bird Designs. $400-500. Indian Post collection.

Matching squash blossom necklace, two bracelets, ring, and earrings with turquoise set in each piece. $1000-1200. Private collection.

Two necklace and earring sets: one with channel-set stones by EJB, Zuni. $165
One with turquoise, shell, coral, and black $185-250

Set of earrings and pendant necklace with sunface channel inlay designs in sterling silver by Jimmy Harrison. Courtesy of Palms Trading Company, Albuquerque. $195-225

Turquoise channel inlay set including cufflinks, ring, watchband (with Seiko watch), bolo tie, small cufflinks, earrings, and tie tac made by Sheldon and Nancy Westika, Zuni, 1986. $400-500 set. Private collection.

Assembled channel inlay set including a bolo tie slide made by Emma Bonney. / Buckle by R.H.C. / Cufflinks and ring by Dickie and Amy Quandelacy, Zuni. / Tie tac by Sheldon and Nancy Westika, Zuni. $300-400 set. Private collection.

Index

A.B., 38
Aguilar, Benny, 4
Aguilar, Mary, 25
Ajax mine, 12
American Turquoise Company, 6
Anjex mine, 12
Apache, 15
Australia, 14
AZ 3AP-TP, 59
Aztecs, 5
B.B., 52
B.H., 38
B.P., 43
Ballow, Luciano, 29
Banteah, Valentino and Matilda, 55
Battle Mountain, 11
Begay, F.M., 23
Begay, Victor M., 39
Benally, David, 58
Benally, Kee, 17
Bisbee mine, 7
Bisbee turquoise, 9, 30, 31, 38, 41, 53
Bitsui and Russell, 51
Blue Diamond mine, 12
Blue Gem mine, 11
Blue Gem turquoise, 13, 15, 31, 45, 49
Blue Jay mine, 12
Blue Stone mine, 12
Bluebird mine, 12
Bonney, Emma, 63
bow guards, 11, 33
Burnham mine, 12
Burro Mountains, 6
Bya, Robert Lee, 51
C. and K., 43
C.H., 37
Calavaza, Wayne, 48
Candeleria mine, 12
Carico Lake mine, 11
Carico Lake turquoise, 13
Carlin mine, 11
Carlin turquoise, 31, 53
Castillian mine, 6
Castle Dome mine, 7
Castle Dome turquoise, 31
Cerillos turquoise, 5, 6, 30, 31, 45
channel inlay, 20, 37, 43, 46, 62, 63
Charley, Y and R., 42, 53
Chee, 54
Chichen Itza, 5
Chile, 14
China, 14
Chinese turquoise, 38
chip turquoise inlay, 21

concha belts, 46, 48
Contention mine, 11
Corbet, Joe, 2
Cortez mine, 11
Cripple Creek mine, 11
Crow Springs mine, 12
D.S.J., 11
Darlene mine, 11
Darling mine, 11
DEB, 39
Dishta, V., 17
Dodge family, 21
Dry Creek mine, 12
E., 52
Easter Blue mine, 12
Easter Blue turquoise, 30
Edaakie, Lee, 53, 59
Egypt, 5, 15
EJB, 62
Emsato, Glenda, 4
Fox mine, 11
Gaussoin, Connie Tsosie, 33
Gaussoin, David, 7, 11, 18, 49, 52
Gaussoin, Wayne Nez, 11
Gem mine, 12
Godber mine, 12
Gonzalez, Pete, 36
Gray, Harold, 49
Hachita Mountains, 6
Hamone, Clifton, 54
Harrison, Jimmy, 62
heishe, 24-26, 29
Hidden Valley turquoise, 11
Homesite mine, 12
Howelite, 5
Hubble, Juan Lorenzo, 5
imitation turquoise, 5
Indian Mountain turquoise, 41, 49
inlay decorations, 18
J.R.D., 42
Jake, C., 60
Jake, Harry, 56
Jim, Thomas, 58
Johnson, C., 45
Johnson, Peterson, 10, 17
Kalestewa, Sue Ellen, 54
ketoh, 11, 33
King Manassa turquoise, 10, 51
King turquoise, 10, 11
King, I.P., 11
Kingman mine, 7, 27
Kingman turquoise, 2, 8, 9, 34, 39, 51, 53, 59
Kirk, Andy, 21
L.M., 45
L.W., 22
Lacco, W., 39
Lander Blue mine, 11

Lander Blue turquoise, 42
Last Chance mine, 12
Leadville, 11
Leekity, T. & L., 51
Leekya, Bernice and Robert, 8
Leekya, S., 43
Lesence, Douglas, 34
Levato, Lupe, 28
Lister, D.K., 2
Lone Mountain turquoise, 11, 12, 24=26, 36, 41
M.F.C., 51
Maisel, 5
Manassa turquoise, 10, 11
marriage crown, 27
Martinez, Ethel, 2
Mayan, 5
McGinnis mine, 12
Medina, Rose, 29
Mexico City, 5
Mexico, 14
Montezuma mine, 12
Morenci turquoise, 7, 8, 15, 30, 31, 34, 36, 39, 41, 46
Mount Chalchihuiti, 6
Mount Taylor, 15
needlepoint turquoise, 4, 20, 22, 36, 39, 44
Nevada Blue turquoise, 48
Nez, Al, 14
Nez, Gibson, 38, 51, 53
Nez, Ned, 51
No. 8 mine, 11
No. 8 turquoise, 11, 45, 60
Ohmsatte, E., 52
Ohmsatte, T., 43
P.H.Y., 49
P.K.H., 37
Padilla, Rita, 13
Panteah, Rosemary, 39, 48, 54
Papoose mine, 12
Paul, Stover, 58
Persian turquoise, 5, 14, 45, 46
Peru, 14
Petit point turquoise, 22, 36, 46, 48, 54, 55
Pilot mine, 12
Pilot Mountain turquoise, 11
Pinto Valley mine, 7
Platero family, 42
Platero, Albert, 44, 57
Platero, Johnson, 13
Pueblo Bonito, 5
Quam, Alice, 49
Quam, Bonnie, 36
Quam, W.V., 52
Quandelacy, 43
Quandelacy, Dickie and Amy, 63
Quintana, Joseph H., 51

R.H.C., 63
R.N.L., 51
rainbow calsilica, 5
Red Mountain turquoise, 11
Royal Blue mine, 12
Royston turquoise, 12, 30, 31
S.D., 21
Sandoval, Felecita, 7
Santa Rita, 6
Seoutewa, E.C., 37
Seowaqseow, 22
Shirley, Mike, 59
Simplicio, Dan, 51
Sleeping Beauty turquoise, 1, 7
Smokey Mountain turquoise, 13
Smokey Valley turquoise, 12, 36
snake eyes, 22
Stone Cabin mine, 11
Stormy Mountain mine, 11
Stormy Mountain turquoise, 12
Stungaten, Paul, 33
Tenorio, Flora, 61
Tibetan turquoise, 14
Tiffany mine, 6
Timberline mine, 11
Tracey, Ray, 21
Tsosie, Boyd, 41
Tsosie, M., 33
Turpen, Tobe, 45, 51, 55, 59
Turquoise Hill, 6
turquoise inlay, 32
Turquoise Mountain tourquoise, 44
Turquoise Tunnel mine, 11
Tuscarara turquoise, 25
V.M.B., 51
Valley Blue mine, 11
Villa Grove mine, 11
Villa Grove turquoise, 31, 46
W.M., 51
Weebothee, Lee and Mary, 41
Westika, Sheldon and Nancy, 63
Wetherill, Marietta, 26
White, Jerry, 17
Willeta, Lolli, 53
Willie, Lonnie, 5, 11
Yazzi, Chee, 16, 51
Yazzie, Lee, 41, 55
Yazzi, Jr., Willie, 23
Yescerva, Cheryl Marie, 49
Yucatan, 5
Zuni pueblo, 15
Zuni, J.B., 37